I0021493

Council Special Report No. 83
November 2018

Zero Botnets
Building a Global Effort to
Clean Up the Internet

Jason Healey and Robert K. Knake

The Council on Foreign Relations (CFR) is an independent, nonpartisan membership organization, think tank, and publisher dedicated to being a resource for its members, government officials, business executives, journalists, educators and students, civic and religious leaders, and other interested citizens in order to help them better understand the world and the foreign policy choices facing the United States and other countries. Founded in 1921, CFR carries out its mission by maintaining a diverse membership, with special programs to promote interest and develop expertise in the next generation of foreign policy leaders; convening meetings at its headquarters in New York and in Washington, DC, and other cities where senior government officials, members of Congress, global leaders, and prominent thinkers come together with Council members to discuss and debate major international issues; supporting a Studies Program that fosters independent research, enabling CFR scholars to produce articles, reports, and books and hold roundtables that analyze foreign policy issues and make concrete policy recommendations; publishing *Foreign Affairs*, the preeminent journal on international affairs and U.S. foreign policy; sponsoring Independent Task Forces that produce reports with both findings and policy prescriptions on the most important foreign policy topics; and providing up-to-date information and analysis about world events and American foreign policy on its website, CFR.org.

The Council on Foreign Relations takes no institutional positions on policy issues and has no affiliation with the U.S. government. All views expressed in its publications and on its website are the sole responsibility of the author or authors.

Council Special Reports (CSRs) are concise policy briefs, produced to provide a rapid response to a developing crisis or contribute to the public's understanding of current policy dilemmas. CSRs are written by individual authors—who may be CFR fellows or acknowledged experts from outside the institution—in consultation with an advisory committee, and are intended to take sixty days from inception to publication. The committee serves as a sounding board and provides feedback on a draft report. It usually meets twice—once before a draft is written and once again when there is a draft for review; however, advisory committee members, unlike Task Force members, are not asked to sign off on the report or to otherwise endorse it. Once published, CSRs are posted on CFR.org.

For further information about CFR or this Special Report, please write to the Council on Foreign Relations, 58 East 68th Street, New York, NY 10065, or call the Communications office at 212.434.9888. Visit our website, CFR.org.

To submit a letter in response to a Council Special Report for publication on our website, CFR.org, you may send an email to publications@cfr.org. Alternatively, letters may be mailed to us at: Publications Department, Council on Foreign Relations, 58 East 68th Street, New York, NY 10065. Letters should include the writer's name, postal address, and daytime phone number. Letters may be edited for length and clarity, and may be published online. Please do not send attachments. All letters become the property of the Council on Foreign Relations and will not be returned. We regret that, owing to the volume of correspondence, we cannot respond to every letter.

CONTENTS

FOREWORD

Cyberspace increasingly resembles nothing so much as the old American Wild West, with no real sheriff and with botnets as the outlaws with guns. Botnets, or groups of computers infected with malicious software that are controlled as a single network, enable much of the internet's cybercrime. They do so by allowing those who control the network to harness supercomputing-level power for nefarious purposes. Botnets are used to spread spam, send phishing emails, guess passwords, break encryption, and launch distributed denial of service attacks. Despite high-profile efforts to eliminate botnets, their number has continued to increase.

As Jason Healey and Robert K. Knake argue in this new Council Special Report, the conventional wisdom that botnets are a problem to be managed aims too low. Botnets can cause serious harm by allowing foreign governments to stifle free speech abroad and enabling them to shut down countries' domestic networks or even the internet globally. Additionally, the economic harm botnets cause is likely to increase significantly over time as the number of internet-connected devices surges. Thus, policymakers should increase their ambition and seek to rid the world of botnets. While having zero botnets may be impossible, the authors conclude that setting such an ambitious target is necessary to focus policy.

The authors propose several innovative policy prescriptions. They suggest policymakers should work to establish the principle that states are responsible for the harm that botnets based within their borders cause to others. Internet service providers should hold each other accountable for the bad traffic leaving their networks. Incentives should be introduced so the makers of internet-connected devices take steps to secure their devices. Components of the internet ecosystem that are used by botnets should be pressured to police themselves and prevent their services from being used for criminal purposes. Finally, an international effort to take down botnets may be necessary should these measures fail to arrest their growth.

The prevalence of botnets and the problems they cause presents further evidence that many of the challenges of the twenty-first century cannot be contained within borders or addressed at the national level. Instead, to minimize botnets' ability to do harm, countries should apply the concept of sovereign obligation, or the notion that sovereign states have not only rights but also obligations vis-à-vis other countries. Governments would have the obligation not just to avoid engaging in prohibited activities but also to do everything in their power to prevent other parties from carrying out those activities from their territory. If countries were to assume such responsibilities, the world would move closer to meeting the target of zero botnets, something that would be in the interest of any entity with a benign agenda.

Richard N. Haass
President
Council on Foreign Relations
November 2018

ACKNOWLEDGMENTS

We would like to thank our advisory committee for sharing their decades of experience. While we are responsible for the content and recommendations of this report, many of the ideas and sources were first presented by advisory committee members. Spamhaus provided invaluable access to their data on botnets, and Justin Haner at Northeastern University made sense of it. We would also like to thank Matt Carothers and Gabriel Ramsey for providing their deep perspectives and experience.

Jason Healey and Robert K. Knake

INTRODUCTION

Botnets are the bane of the internet. Criminals use these groups of computers infected with malicious software to propagate spam, send phishing emails, guess passwords, impersonate users, and break encryption. Their most pernicious use, however, is to carry out distributed denial of service (DDoS) attacks. DDoS attacks harness the power of the individual computers that make up the botnet to send internet traffic to a target, thereby blocking legitimate traffic. As much as 30 percent of all internet traffic may be attributable to botnets, and most of that traffic is from DDoS attacks.[1]

Most DDoS attacks are criminal in nature, often used by companies to take down their competitors' websites or servers; however, China, Russia, and Iran have all harnessed botnets for geopolitical purposes. China has carried out DDoS attacks against the *New York Times*, the Falun Gong, and Chinese Christian churches in the United States. Russia carried out DDoS attacks through proxies against Estonia in 2007, following Estonia's removal of a statue commemorating Russian soldiers in Tallinn, and in 2008, in conjunction with Russia's military operations against Georgia. Iran carried out a series of sustained, large-scale attacks against the U.S. financial sector from 2011 to 2013 in response to alleged U.S. action against its nuclear program. These attacks reportedly cost some banks upward of $20 million per month to keep their websites available to customers.

Conventional wisdom is that botnets and the problems they create need to be "managed"—that botnets and the harm that they cause are, though a problem, simply part of an open and global internet. Interventions to reduce botnet infections will, therefore, end up harming the vibrancy of the internet, hurting innovation, and stifling freedom. This view is wrong for three reasons.

First, it fails to take seriously the harm to society created when foreign governments directly attack protected freedoms by stifling free speech in the United States. That the U.S. government has appeared powerless to do anything to stop them should be of great concern. When the website of technology reporter Brian Krebs was taken offline by a DDoS attack, Krebs was only able to get his website back online once Google took over and absorbed the attack through its Project Shield program.[2] Relying on a private company with profit motives to protect free speech in the United States, and globally, raises concerns.

Second, a motivated nation-state actor could easily harness millions of systems to shut down countries' domestic networks or target core internet infrastructure and shut the internet down globally. For foreign governments, there are certainly scenarios where they might judge such actions to be to their advantage.

Finally, while the economic harms may be manageable today, they likely will not be tomorrow. Cybercrime today may cost the global economy $600 billion per year, with much of that loss tied to botnets, and those losses are only set to grow.[3] The internet of things (IoT) is leading to massive growth in the number of internet-connected devices. These devices are often not built with security in mind and are rarely updated once installed, resulting in known vulnerabilities that can be exploited by adversaries but are unlikely to be patched. They are therefore more likely to be vulnerable to takeover as part of a botnet, and the infection is less likely to be discovered and remediated. In 2016, the Mirai botnet knocked the domain-name service provider Dyn offline along with many of its clients, including Airbnb, Amazon, GitHub, HBO, Netflix, PayPal, and Twitter. Criminals carried out the attack with just a fraction of the bots they had at their control.

Harnessing even a small percentage of vulnerable IoT devices would give a malicious actor the ability to flood the internet with traffic that could disrupt core functions. As the remaining three billion people who are not yet on the internet come online, the infection rates of these users' IoT devices are likely to be high. About sixteen billion devices are connected to the internet today, and both that number and the number of vulnerable and infected devices are expected to double in the next five years. Even if only the tiniest fraction of these devices is infected with botnets, malicious actors will have enormous disruptive potential at their disposal. Thus an ambitious goal of zero botnets is necessary.

To achieve that goal, information security experts first need to do a better job of measuring current botnet activity and set incremental goals for reductions. Nations and international institutions should then work to establish the principle that states are responsible for the harm that botnets based within their borders cause to others. When governments are unable or unwilling to be responsible, other states may be justified in taking action, in or out of the cyber domain, to thwart cross-border effects. Similarly, at the internet service provider (ISP) level, good stewards of online spaces need to hold other ISPs accountable for the bad traffic leaving their networks. The makers of devices that are vulnerable to becoming parts of botnets need to be incentivized to secure their devices, and the resellers of those devices should use their leverage to hold them accountable. Hosting providers, name registrars, and other components of the internet ecosystem that are used by botnets should be pressured to police themselves and prevent their services from being used for criminal purposes. Finally, when these measures fail to suppress the growth of botnets, an ongoing international effort to take down botnets is necessary.

THE POWER OF ZERO

Zero is a powerful concept often used as a tool to galvanize policy action. Setting a target of zero for undesirable outcomes signals that any occurrence is unacceptable. As progress is made, occurrences become exceptions that trigger forceful responses to understand what went wrong and prevent the same patterns from being repeated.

In the aviation industry, no passenger on a U.S.-registered commercial airline had been killed as the result of a crash or accident in over nine years until the recent death of a passenger on Southwest Flight 1380 in April 2018. That incident triggered a thorough review of engine safety and the protocols by which engine safety is confirmed. For the flying public, regulators, airline stockholders, and operators, zero is the only acceptable number of safety incidents.

Policymakers are taking a similar approach in areas such as traffic accidents and public health policy. The mayors of Los Angeles, New York, Washington, DC, and thirty other cities are pursuing so-called Vision Zero programs for traffic and pedestrian fatalities. The effort is based on a program begun in Sweden twenty years ago. In the public health domain, multiple vaccination efforts aim for zero infections worldwide. Smallpox vaccination efforts successfully reached the goal of zero new infections in 1978. Efforts to combat polio have resulted in just twenty-two new infections worldwide in 2017.

Of course, completely eliminating botnets is likely an impossible goal. Similarly, the world is unlikely to ever get to zero nuclear weapons (the goal of the Global Zero movement embraced by President Barack Obama in 2009), just as Sweden, New York City, and Washington, DC, are not likely to have zero traffic deaths (the goal of Vision Zero). But sometimes an extreme goal is necessary to focus policy. As the data shows, extremely low infection rates (less than 0.1 percent in the United States today) can still allow for powerful botnets to be assembled. Thus, infection rates need to be driven well below that number to effectively zero.

MEASURING THE CURRENT STATE OF BOTNET INFECTIONS

Botnet infections vary greatly across the globe, with extremely low infection rates in undeveloped countries, high rates in developing countries, and low and improving rates of infection in the developed world. In the developed world, some countries have taken active steps to drive botnet infections to nearly zero. Notably, Finland has an active and voluntary partnership with its ISPs to notify the owners of infected systems and, if necessary, quarantine them. Finland consistently has one of the lowest infection rates among developed countries. Other national efforts have been less effective. Japan created its Cyber Clean Center in 2008 to reduce infection rates but, by most metrics, continues to have a significant botnet problem. Germany has led a multiyear effort to reduce domestic botnet infections, but its approach is nowhere near as effective as Finland's. The United States, without a coordinated national approach or a legal requirement, compares favorably to many other countries that have such approaches or requirements. Data provided by Spamhaus, an international organization that tracks botnet activities, places the United States at number fourteen on the list of countries with the most botnet infections (see table 1).

Table 1. COUNTRIES WITH THE MOST BOTNET INFECTIONS

Rank (most to least infected)	Country	Average number of bots
1	China	1,976,804
2	India	1,689,265
3	Brazil	606,216
4	Iran	566,353
5	Vietnam	560,720
6	Russia	506,982
7	Thailand	419,979
8	Turkey	412,390
9	Mexico	360,876
10	Indonesia	317,988
11	Pakistan	201,315
12	Philippines	166,177
13	Venezuela	156,718
14	United States	154,719
15	Egypt	148,298
16	Algeria	145,273
17	Japan	142,461
18	Italy	115,546
19	Argentina	113,470
20	Malaysia	101,093

Source: Spamhaus, 2018.

However, on a per capita basis, U.S. networks are among the cleanest in the world. Among Organization for Economic Cooperation and Development (OECD) countries, the United States has the eighth-cleanest network (see table 2), possibly due to lower rates of pirated or unsupported software and the prevalence of antivirus software. Germany comes in at twelve on the list, Japan at sixteen.[4]

Yet in light of the past and potential harm that botnets cause, even infection rates that are well below one-tenth of 1 percent are too high, given the large and growing number of systems on the internet. Although the United States has an infection rate that is among the lowest in the world, the country was also one of the top five source countries for DDoS attacks in each quarter of 2017 (see table 3).[5] Thus, managing the botnet problem requires driving the absolute number of infections to or near zero.

Table 2. RANKING OF BOTNET INFECTION RATES AMONG TWENTY OECD COUNTRIES

Rank (least to most infected)	Country	% of IP addresses infected
1	Denmark	0.0258%
1	Finland	0.0258%
2	Switzerland	0.0353%
3	Netherlands	0.0549%
4	France	0.0574%
5	United Kingdom	0.0583%
6	Canada	0.0608%
7	Belgium	0.0627%
8	United States	0.0629%
9	Estonia	0.0816%
10	New Zealand	0.0830%
11	Sweden	0.0835%
12	Germany	0.1039%
13	Austria	0.1079%
14	Korea	0.1123%
15	Iceland	0.1171%
16	Japan	0.1204%
17	Luxembourg	0.1430%
18	Slovakia	0.1447%
19	Czech Republic	0.1509%

Source: Spamhaus, 2018.

Table 3. TOP FIVE SOURCE COUNTRIES FOR DDoS ATTACKS, *2017*

Q4 2017		Q3 2017		Q2 2017		Q1 2017	
Country	Percentage / Source IPs	Country	Percentage / Source IPs	Country	Percentage / Source IPs	Country	Percentage / Source IPs
Germany	30% / 128,350	Germany	22% / 58,746	Egypt	32% / 44,198	United States	44% / 594,986
China	28% / 118,716	United States	14% / 38,628	United States	8% / 11,113	United Kingdom	13% / 177,579
United States	8% / 36,441	India	7% / 19,722	Turkey	5% / 7,049	Germany	7% / 87,780
Ecuador	3% / 14,685	China	6% / 15,323	China	4% / 5,711	Canada	5% / 60,581
Austria	3% / 13,503	Mexico	5% / 13,501	India	4% / 5,224	Brazil	3% / 43,863

Source: McKeay, "State of the Internet / Security: Q4 2017 Report."

WHY BOTNETS PERSIST

Despite high-profile efforts to tackle botnets, the number of botnets and infected systems only continues to grow. Past efforts have been disjointed and focused separately on either ISP notifications to owners of infected systems or coordinated law enforcement efforts to arrest so-called botmasters and disrupt the infrastructure they use to control their botnets.

The Federal Communications Commission (FCC) worked with the major ISPs under the Communications Security, Reliability, and Interoperability Council (CSRIC) to produce the Anti-Bot Code of Conduct in 2012.[6] This code is a voluntary effort to educate customers on botnets, detect botnet activities, notify customers of suspected infection, and provide information on how to remediate botnet infections. While many ISPs adopted the practices promoted in the code of conduct, their effectiveness remains unclear.

In April 2013, the FBI announced Operation Clean Slate, which had the stated goal of reducing or eliminating botnets that threatened the economic security of the United States and the privacy of its citizens.[7] Although the FBI enjoyed a string of successes in shutting down some botnets, these efforts have not led to a measurable reduction in the number of botnets, the number of infected devices, or the harm that botnets cause.

A more comprehensive approach beyond law enforcement and ISP notification and quarantine is necessary to addresses the problem from multiple vectors. The challenges of eliminating botnets stem from three categories: existing and new technologies; operational, organizational, and process issues; and policy and economics.

The ease of spoofing. Criminals leading DDoS attacks take advantage of every opportunity to cover their tracks and make it difficult for responders to identify the source of the attack. Because DDoS attacks do not require two-way communication and instead simply flood the victim with traffic, botmasters often program their malware to "spoof," or fake, the internet protocol (IP) address that data packets originate from—i.e., make it look like the data is coming from a different address—so it is difficult to identify the sources of the attack. The United States has the largest number of spoofable IP blocks, but these represent just 4.8 percent of all its IP addresses in sample data. In many developing countries, 100 percent of IP blocks are spoofable.[8] In the late 1990s, members of the internet security community developed a protocol to address this problem, called Best Common Practice 38. The protocol called on ISPs to implement "egress filtering," in which any packets claiming to be from IP addresses that they had not been assigned are blocked.

Bulletproof hosting. Bulletproof hosting providers are those that host criminal activity that legitimate hosting companies will not abide. No improved system of abuse reporting will change how bulletproof hosting providers operate. They are often located in countries with weak law enforcement, high levels of corruption, or poor relations with the West. Often offering services at low cost, these providers claim that they do not have the resources to police users' content or respond to every report of abuse. Because they almost always host some legitimate businesses that are drawn by cut-rate services, shutting them down outright or stopping all traffic coming from them is not an appropriate response.

The growth of IoT. IoT technologies make managing the botnet problem more difficult. The sheer number of devices means that even a low rate of infection can give malicious actors access to incredibly large numbers of compromised devices. Moreover, the "set and forget" nature of these devices means that owners are less likely to install software updates or otherwise secure their devices. Much of the predicted growth in IoT devices is because they are inexpensive, which leads to poor development practices and thus less secure devices. Furthermore, 60 percent of all internet applications contain open-source components with known software vulnerabilities.[9]

The emergence of cryptocurrencies. Much of the value that criminals gain from operating botnets and DDoS extortion schemes comes from cryptocurrencies such as bitcoin and ethereum. Criminals will begin a DDoS attack and then demand a payment in cryptocurrency to stop it—typically far less than a DDoS mitigation firm would charge. Cryptocurrencies allow criminals to demand ransom payments that are not easily traced through the financial system—gone are the days of unmarked briefcases of nonsequential $100 bills. Although all bitcoin transactions are publicly recorded in the associated blockchain, the individuals associated with these transactions are unknown by design. The development of "tumbling" services that combine noncriminal cryptocurrency transactions with criminal ones makes it difficult for law enforcement to target remaining vulnerable points in the system, such as when criminals seek to convert virtual currencies to fiat currencies. Newer currencies like monero, zcash, and dash are seemingly designed expressly for criminal transactions.[10]

OPERATIONAL, ORGANIZATIONAL, AND PROCESS ISSUES

The complexity of botnet takedowns. Coordinated takedowns of botnets by law enforcement, ISPs, software companies, security firms, and academia can dramatically reduce the number of infected machines worldwide and the associated ills. Yet maintaining persistent efforts over time has proven difficult. Botnet takedowns are no one's full-time job. In a ten-year period, twenty-three partial or total botnet takedowns occurred (see table 4). Takedowns proceed in fits and starts: 2012 saw four botnet takedowns, followed by three in 2013, one in 2014, three in 2015, one in 2016, and two in 2017.[11] The most effective takedowns involve a wide array of parties that act in concert to attack the botnet from multiple angles: court orders are used to seize servers and web domains globally, law enforcement arrests known and accessible members of the criminal organization behind the botnet, ISPs sinkhole traffic, software vendors push patches, and, under law enforcement authority, technical experts attempt to take over or delete the underlying malware all at once.

Leadership of these efforts has been diffuse. No single organization is responsible for coordinating takedowns. Microsoft alone has pursued more than a dozen. Cybersecurity firms including CrowdStrike, FireEye, Lastline, Symantec, and TrendMicro have led other efforts. The FBI, the U.S. Department of Justice, and the Secret Service have also coordinated efforts. Formal and informal third-party

Table 4. MAJOR BOTNET TAKEDOWNS OF THE PAST DECADE

Date	Botnet
November 2008	McColo
November 2009	Mega D
December 2009	Mariposa
February 2010	Waledac
September 2010	Pushdo
November 2010	DNSCHanger
March 2011	Rustock
April 2011	Coreflood
November 2011	Rove Digital
March 2012	Zeus Botnet
July 2012	Grum
September 2012	Nitol
December 2012	Butterfly Bot
February 2013	Bamital
June 2013	Citadel
December 2013	Sirefef/ZeroAccess
June 2014	Gameover Zeus
February 2015	Ramnit
April 2015	Simda
December 2015	Dorkbot
December 2016	Avalanche
April 2017	Kelihos Botnet
December 2017	Gamarue/Andromeda

Source: Authors' research.

organizations, including Europol's European Cybercrime Center, the Internet Systems Consortium, Malware Anti-Abuse Working Group, Mariposa Working Group, National Cyber Forensics Training Alliance, and Spamhaus have coordinated takedowns. These efforts draw on a limited pool of technical talent and strain the resources of the organizations that contribute to the effort. In short, botnet takedowns are no one's day job.

Broken processes for abuse reporting. Processes for reporting DDoS attacks, other malicious activity, and vulnerable systems are broken. Hosting providers and ISPs often ignore abuse reports or address them only slowly. Effectively reporting abuse often relies on an informal—and not always effective—network of individuals at companies that span the globe. The efforts of one victim of Mirai illustrate this problem well: As the attack against ProxyPipe, a DDoS mitigation provider for Minecraft servers, continued, Robert Coelho, the company's vice president, was unable to keep his clients' servers accessible. He resorted to filing abuse complaints with the hosting providers and ISPs that supported the botmaster's command-and-control server that directed the attack. Coelho concluded that the control server was being run out of a notorious bulletproof hosting provider in Ukraine. That provider, BlazingFast, did not respond to abuse reports from Coelho, nor did BlazingFast's DDoS mitigation service, Voxility. Coelho then contacted four upstream ISPs that provided no assistance before a fifth ISP, the Finnish TeliaSonera, responded to his request and shut down the control server's connectivity over its network. "The action by Telia cut the size of the attacks launched by the botnet down to 80 Gbps," a level of traffic that ProxyPipe could manage.[12]

Yet a faster, automated system for abuse reporting could create its own problems. Even for companies that intend to be good stewards of cyberspace, such a system could result in the equivalent of "swatting" online, where abuse systems are misused to shut down legitimate activity.[13] Some companies have developed verified networks among trusted parties to automate this process. Hosting providers and ISPs that are not responsive face few repercussions. Lacking any third-party recourse, victims of malicious activity are on their own to work with often indifferent and hostile corporations.

Poor mechanisms for international cooperation. The role of national computer emergency response teams (CERTs) is ill-defined within the internet ecosystem: only some have the ability to provide assistance to foreign governments and foreign corporations. In countries with national telecommunications providers and laws that favor notification and quarantine, national CERTs play a useful role. In the United States, the Computer Emergency Readiness Team has only a limited ability to assist in the event of a DDoS attack.

The difficulty of identifying infected system owners. When network defenders are able to trace infected or vulnerable systems back to the networks where they are located, they often are only able to go as far as the ISP that is providing service. In the United States, ISPs are not permitted to share information about their customers with third parties based on statutory language in the Electronic Communications Privacy Act (ECPA). This prohibition extends to government agencies unless a law enforcement subpoena is issued. Internationally, identification of system owners is also hampered by local laws such as the Global Data Protection Regulation (GDPR) in the European Union. Now coming into force, GDPR treats IP addresses as personal data that is subject to protection. Thus efforts to notify the owner of the system and encourage remediation action need to rely on the ISP (unless the system is on the network of a large corporation with its own address space). Many ISPs have been reluctant to notify customers actively of infections due to costs and privacy concerns.

POLICY AND ECONOMIC ISSUES

Economic incentives that favor the attacker. According to cybersecurity expert Jim Lewis, "a botnet costing only $60 a day can inflict as much as $720,000 in damages on victim organizations, and the hackers controlling the botnets enjoy a profit margin of over 70% when renting their services out to other criminals."[14] Interventions that will raise the costs of carrying out these attacks as well as lowering the profits should be identified and implemented.

Perverse incentives for DDoS mitigation. Companies that provide DDoS mitigation services do not want to see the attacks stop—they want them to continue at manageable levels. As Coelho, vice president at ProxyPipe, put it in a text exchange with the botmaster behind Mirai, "We just wanted the attacks to get smaller"—he did not say he wanted the attacks to stop.[15]

DDoS mitigation is a growing business. Companies like Akamai and Cloudflare offer flat-rate services that act like an insurance policy and properly align incentives so mitigation providers have an interest in cleaning up the ecosystem. Feedback loops from DDoS victims to botnet sources could eventually drive down botnet numbers to zero, but they are still a work in progress.

Indirect costs of botnets. Botnets cause harm typically not to the systems they infect but to third parties. Botnets' use of computing resources and bandwidth does not appear to be of significant concern to the owners and operators of most infected systems. Some individuals do not worry about their personal information being stolen and barely notice the performance hit their computers take while they mine cryptocurrencies for others. Some companies turn a blind eye to the theft of their intellectual property. Yet though botmasters extract whatever value they can from infected systems, the real value in maintaining a botnet is using it to target third parties.

Privacy concerns and a lack of economic incentives for ISP action. Net neutrality has in the past contributed to ISPs' hands-off approach, with ISPs maintaining that as common carriers they are obligated to pass on traffic unless it causes a direct harm to their own systems—not to other ISPs or end users farther downstream. With the FCC's termination of net neutrality rules, ISPs' concern over violating net neutrality by blocking botnet activity has been addressed. Moreover, changes to the ECPA by the Cybersecurity Act of 2015 give ISPs broad exemptions from liability for blocking malicious traffic. The broader problem remains that many ISPs do not see fighting botnets as part of their business model; filtering out DDoS traffic for customers or providing additional bandwidth to victims is good business. ISPs are not likely to embrace blocking their customers' access to the internet, at least in the U.S. market. A more promising approach, which AT&T and CenturyLink are testing, does not try to clean up the infections but instead disrupts their command and control on the network so that the botmaster cannot direct the activities of the bots, rendering the threat from them inert.

RECOMMENDATIONS

In Executive Order 13800, U.S. President Donald J. Trump directed the Department of Commerce and the Department of Homeland Security to work with the private sector to identify ways of "dramatically reducing threats perpetrated by automated and distributed attacks (e.g., botnets)." The ensuing report, "Enhancing the Resilience of the Internet and Communications Ecosystem Against Botnets and Other Automated, Distributed Threats," released in May 2018, is an invaluable resource in defining the problem, and many of its recommendations inform those below.[16] What is missing from this effort that was informed by dozens of organizations with a stake in reducing the threat of botnets is a clear and measurable goal. Establishing a global goal of zero botnets is the first step in addressing the problem.

From there, national commitments to achieve zero botnets within national networks should be sought. Interim goals and systems to measure progress toward those goals are crucial. Such goals could be addressed primarily within national bounds. Goals should be set over specific time frames based on the number of connected devices within a country. Developed countries should have more stringent requirements and faster time lines, with less onerous initial requirements for developing countries.

SET A GLOBAL GOAL AND MEASURE STATES AGAINST IT

To achieve zero botnets, it is necessary to set interim goals and measure progress against them. Botnet goals should be agreed to by political leaders, along with civil society and the executives of global companies. Setting these goals and having major partners agree to them is the most important first step to creating a movement.

These goals should start with an agreement to target the achievement of zero botnets by major ISPs, which could be as simple as a podium handshake by the presidents of the United States and China. A larger community can then develop more concrete metrics, norms, and implementation. Those involved can course-correct as they see successes and failures in meeting these milestones, and harvest lessons learned from countries and companies that succeed. Agreeing on metrics and measuring success against them will be difficult. Spamhaus and other organizations have been tracking botnets and infection rates by country for years.[17] Likewise, the Cyber Green Initiative has been working to track botnets scientifically.[18] Such groups can measure the progress toward zero botnets.

ESTABLISH THE PRINCIPLE OF STATE RESPONSIBILITY FOR THE HARMS CAUSED BY BOTNETS

As twenty-first-century challenges like terrorism, nuclear proliferation, and pollution have become national security challenges, notions of national sovereignty have also changed. Rather than being an absolute right of states, sovereignty now comes with sovereign responsibility to the citizens of states and sovereign obligations to other states.[19] Botnets cause harm to individuals, to companies, and to states, but only when the harm is cross-border in nature does it become an international policy concern, in which the state causing the harm has a sovereign obligation to other states to address it.[20] By this line of reasoning, states could choose to allow high rates of botnet infections as long as the harm they cause is limited to their own territory. They should, however, be held liable by the international system for any harm caused to other states if they are not proactively and cooperatively working to respond to it.

ENCOURAGE INTERNATIONAL COOPERATION AND ACTION

States should have both carrot and stick inducements for taking action to reduce the prevalence of botnets on their national networks. Placing states on a spectrum of responsibility may be useful. First would be states that are actively using botnets to coerce other states: these should be specifically targeted by international institutions. Next would be states that harbor the criminal enterprises behind botnet operations. States that are simply unable to police what is happening inside their borders would be on the bottom of the spectrum.

With this framework in mind, incentives could then be used to help those on the bottom end of the spectrum achieve reductions. Penalties such as shaming, limiting investment, and sanctions could target those states that are actively using botnets or harboring those that do. Developed states will need to provide support to developing nations for reducing botnet activity, including by helping address long-standing problems in the ecosystem, such as the prevalence of pirated software. The U.S. government, like-minded nations, and corporations with an interest in reducing botnet activity should fund an annual report by an independent third-party organization to track state-level success in reducing botnets.

Once international obligations are set up, failure to respond could provide reasonable grounds for nations to take limited action to prevent, in the narrowest way possible, the harm without causing more harm in return. For instance, in the event that a country fails to establish mechanisms to receive and act on abuse complaints in a timely fashion, a foreign government could authorize the takedown of a command-and-control server. Taking actions such as this should be done as a last resort given that states might perceive them as a violation of sovereignty and a hostile action, no matter how limited.

CREATE INCENTIVES FOR ISPS TO CLEAN UP NETWORKS

Some ISPs detect when a customer is infected with malware, notify that person by text, and then divert them to a "walled garden" where they are unable to access the wider internet until the computer is cleaned, sometimes with help from the ISP. Critically, it is not the person who is barred from the internet, as that would limit free speech, but rather the device that is causing harm to others. Yet although this practice has been in place for a over a decade, it is not accepted as a common responsibility of ISPs.

Although ISPs are wary of regulation in this space, ISPs as a community could self-police. ISPs could agree to a standard wherein, for instance, an ISP with one hundred million devices or a petabyte of traffic a month could be allowed a certain percentage of infected devices, or emissions. If the ISP had more than that, it would have to pay a fee or buy credits from a cleaner network until it was able to bring the number down below the threshold.

SET STANDARDS TO KEEP DEVICES FROM BEING EASILY COMPROMISED

As the report to the president concludes, "Performance-based security capability baselines—which identify suites of voluntary standards, specifications, and security mechanisms that represent the combination of best practices for lifecycle security for a particular threat environment—are needed to accelerate the development and deployment of IoT devices and systems that are less vulnerable to compromise throughout their lifecycles."[21] What the report does not do is identify who should develop these standards; yet the National Institute of Standards and Technology (NIST) has already completed much of the preliminary work to produce such standards and has an excellent track record of working with industry. The president or secretary of commerce should direct NIST to quickly establish standards for IoT device security. These standards should include the following.

- *Eliminating known vulnerabilities at the time of production.* Open-source components should be the most updated versions, and device manufacturers should scan for vulnerabilities in the code they write.

- *Following best practices for device hardening.* The standards should also require manufacturers to put in place measures that make it more difficult for adversaries to compromise devices.

- *Making devices updatable.* New operational technology is likely to persist in the environment far longer than office technology, so it is crucial that IoT devices have the capacity for remote and automatic updates to address security flaws. Such updates should be automated by default, with users able to choose to test updates before deployment.

- *Maintaining a "bill of materials" for software components.* As vulnerabilities are discovered in open-source components, owners of technology should know whether software has been built with secure components.

- *Providing unique passwords for each device.* Entire production runs of IoT devices often use the same default passwords. Changing this procedure would eliminate the easiest method attackers use to gain control of devices.[22]

USE MARKET PRESSURE TO INCENTIVIZE DEVICE MAKERS TO MEET STANDARDS

Just as cars cannot be sold if they pollute excessively, resellers should refuse to sell products that have not been demonstrated to be secure. *Consumer Reports* and other organizations are developing cybersecurity ratings for electronic devices.[23] This effort will take time to mature but is the right mechanism to reduce the spread of insecure devices. If done right, it can better align markets and incentives at low cost but with great effect.

Beyond transparency, retailers should refuse to sell products that do not meet the NIST standards. Walmart and Amazon are already the most powerful "regulators" on a host of issues: they specify the size of containers and the shape of packaging they allow. Requiring that IoT devices meet security standards would do more than almost any other action to reduce the prevalence of botnets. BestBuy's decision to cease selling Kaspersky Lab's antivirus software following U.S. government claims that it was tied to Kremlin spying is a precedent for such action.

Similar actions on insecure devices could have a significant effect. Banks, often the victims of DDoS attacks, should apply pressure on device makers and resellers by refusing to lend to companies that do not meet standards. Regulators for critical infrastructure should ban devices that do not meet the standard. Although in the current political climate it is unlikely that new regulatory powers will be granted, regulators with existing authority should set this requirement.

CALL OUT ENABLERS OF BOTNET ACTIVITY

Successful campaigns that employ the concept of zero (e.g., in traffic accidents or plane crashes) actively measure progress and publicize both successes and failures in the attempt to reach that goal. Such transparency could help pressure those responsible for botnet activity.

Cybercriminals often turn to leading cloud-computing services when they need computing resources for command and control of DDoS attacks. In 2017, OVH, the target of DDoS attacks carried out by Mirai, hosted the most botnet command-and-control servers in the world; Amazon hosted the second most.[24] Most of these command-and-control servers were created by simply purchasing the company's services, typically with stolen credit card numbers bought on the dark web. The U.S.-based registrar NameCheap is the most popular place for botnet operators to purchase web addresses for command and control (botnets need to contact web domains to receive instructions). NameCheap accounted for 11,878 registrations for botnet operation in 2017, one-quarter of all such registrations.

Law enforcement, shareholders, and customers could pressure the sellers of cloud computing and web domains favored by cyber criminals to make the operation of botnets much more difficult. Rapidly identifying and removing accounts involved in this criminal activity is well within the technical capability of these firms but, absent pressure to do so, it is not in their financial interest. The United States and allies should also place pressure on countries where this activity germinates through naming and shaming, sanctions, and criminal prosecutions of botmasters and services that allow them to function.

If legitimate service providers police themselves and thus force criminal groups to use providers that knowingly turn a blind eye, it will be possible to isolate and punish these groups. ISPs have in the past blocked such providers from accessing large portions of the internet. Taking these actions more broadly, however, will only be tenable once these groups stand out more from the current high level of malicious activity. ISPs are already experimenting with mechanized ways to drop bad traffic.

ESTABLISH AN INDEPENDENT ORGANIZATION FOR BOTNET TAKEDOWNS

Even when takedowns deliver incredible results, success is usually the output of an outstanding level of work. This should be changed so that takedowns can happen at scale, with the benefits outweighing the input. As one editor explained in a TechTarget blog, "If we determine that a botnet is sending millions of messages a day—the command servers are in Russia, part of the infrastructure is in Spain, and the bots are in North America—there has to be a way for all of these groups to cooperate in real time, or really quickly. Because when you take down a botnet, if you don't take down the whole structure at the same time, it is very easy for these guys to seize control and redirect all that traffic somewhere else."[25]

Botnet takedowns involve high-skilled, time-consuming technical work and are no one's full-time job. But they should be. One possibility would be establishing cyber incident collaboration organizations (CICOs).[26] One such group could focus on each major type of incident, such as counter-DDoS or counter–malware outbreaks. The counter-botnet CICO would be "global and led by the private sector, with membership including the global organizations that have had the largest role in takedowns—such as, say, Microsoft, FireEye, and the Department of Justice." This group would work with related CICOs against malicious software and DDoS attacks, as these are often related. Such groups "cannot simply be a new organization with additional overhead. Rather, the goal of a CICO should be to streamline the current response process for an incident type; to provide an umbrella to make such work easier or to upscale it."[27]

A relatively small organization funded at $10 million per year over a five-year period would likely be capable of carrying out multiple takedowns per year. This organization could also measure botnets globally and provide technical assistance to countries and companies struggling to reduce their infection rates. Funding such an organization could be a challenge, but given the costs that DDoS attacks cause, supporting an organization that reduces the threat would be in the interests of the financial sector, the telecommunications sector, cloud-computing providers, and government agencies.

These groups should be international from their birth, not outgrowths of national cybersecurity bureaucracies. National CERTs should be involved, but the required agility and ease of coordinating across borders is likely to be too difficult for governments to do directly.

CONCLUSION

The threat from botnets to the health of the internet and the modern, digital economy that relies on it only continues to grow. With billions of new devices set to join the internet in the next decade, now is the time to put in place an international regime that works to keep vulnerable devices off the internet, mitigate devices once they have become infected, and respond to the problems that infected devices cause. Absent sustained, organized efforts to combat this problem, botnets and the malicious actors that control them will take an ever-increasing chunk of the value created by the internet and the systems connected to it.

Zero botnets is an effective rallying cry to motivate the disparate coalition of technology makers, ISPs, consumers, cybersecurity companies, nonprofits, and law enforcement organizations that are necessary to reduce botnet infections to levels at which they do not pose a threat to the continued operation of the internet or the organizations that operate on it. If properly motivated, such a coalition could, over time, drive down botnet infection rates, increase the costs to malicious actors to operate them, and deny them value for doing so.

ENDNOTES

1. Joy Ma and Tim Matthews, "The Underground Bot Economy: How Bots Impact the Global Economy," Imperva Incapsula, July 5, 2016, http://incapsula.com/blog/how-bots-impact-global-economy.html.

2. "Project Shield," Google, accessed May 21, 2018, http://projectshield.withgoogle.com/public.

3. James Lewis, "Economic Impact of Cybercrime—No Slowing Down," Center for Strategic and International Studies and McAfee, February 2018, http://mcafee.com/enterprise/en-us/assets/reports/restricted/economic-impact-cybercrime.pdf.

4. Data for tables 1 and 2 provided by Spamhaus for 2018; data analysis completed by Justin Haner, Northeastern University.

5. Martin McKeay, ed., "State of the Internet / Security: Q4 2017 Report," Akamai, http://akamai.com/us/en/multimedia/documents/state-of-the-internet/q4-2017-state-of-the-internet-security-report.pdf.

6. *Final Report: U.S. Anti-Bot Code of Conduct (ABCs) for Internet Service Providers (ISPs)*, Communications Security, Reliability and Interoperability Council (Federal Communications Commission: Washington, DC, 2012), http://m3aawg.org/system/files/20120322-wg7-final-report-for-csric-iii_5.pdf.

7. *Taking Down Botnets*, 113th Cong. (2014) (statement of Joseph Demarest, Assistant Director of the Cyber Division, FBI), http://fbi.gov/news/testimony/taking-down-botnets.

8. Spoofer, "Country Stats for Last Year of Data," Center for Applied Internet Data Analysis, last modified June 8, 2018, http://spoofer.caida.org/country_stats.php.

9. Black Duck Software, "2017 Open Source Security and Risk Analysis," http://blackducksoftware.com/sites/default/files/images/Downloads/Reports/USA/OSSRA17_Rpt_UL.pdf.

10. Kieran Corcoran, "Law Enforcement Has a Massive Problem With These 3 Cryptocurrencies," *Business Insider*, February 27, 2018, http://businessinsider.com/law-enforcement-problems-with-monero-zcash-dash-cryptocurrencies-2018-2.

11. Authors' research.

12. Brian Krebs, "Who Is Anna-Senpai, the Mirai Worm Author?," *Krebs on Security* (blog), January 17, 2018, http://krebsonsecurity.com/2017/01/who-is-anna-senpai -the-mirai-worm-author.

13. Urban Dictionary, s.v. "Swatting," by Droct, August 27, 2014, http://urbandictionary .com/define.php?term=Swatting.

14. Lewis, "Economic Impact of Cybercrime."

15. Krebs, "Who Is Anna-Senpai."

16. U.S. Department of Commerce, U.S. Department of Homeland Security, "A Report to the President on Enhancing the Resilience of the Internet and Communications Ecosystem Against Botnets and Other Automated, Distributed Threats," May 22, 2018, http://commerce.gov/sites/commerce.gov/files/media/files/2018/eo_13800 _botnet_report_-_finalv2.pdf.

17. CBL (Composite Blocking List), "CBL Breakdown by Country, Highest by Count," Spamhaus, accessed April 24, 2018, http://abuseat.org/public/country.html.

18. CyberGreen Institute (website), accessed May 21, 2018, http://cybergreen.net.

19. See Richard Haass, *A World in Disarray: American Foreign Policy and the Crisis of the Old Order* (New York: Penguin Press, 2017).

20. Jason Healey and Hannah Pitts point out that this tension between state sovereignty and international obligation has been addressed in international environmental law "through the articulation of limited state liability for certain acts that originate within the territory of one state that cause harm to another state or to its citizens." Jason Healey and Hannah Pitts, "Applying International Environmental Legal Norms to Cyber Statecraft," *I/S: A Journal of Law and Policy for the Information Society* 8, no. 2 (2012).
    The principle of sovereign obligation is represented in environmental law by cases like the Trail Smelter case, in which a transborder dispute between the United States and Canada involving pollution helped establish the principle that states have an obligation under international law to prevent harm to their neighbors. See Catherine Prunella, "An International Environmental Law Case Study: The Trail Smelter Arbitration," *International Pollution Issues*, December 2014, http://intlpollution.commons.gc.cuny.edu /an-international-environmental-law-case-study-the-trail-smelter-arbitration.

21. U.S. Department of Commerce, U.S. Department of Homeland Security, "A Report to the President."

22. These recommendations draw on the work of I Am the Cavalry, a nonprofit organization dedicated to improving the security of IoT devices. See http://iamthecavalry.org; for a fuller discussion see "Enhancing the Resilience of the Internet": "Action 1.1. Using industry-led inclusive processes, establish internationally applicable IoT capability baselines supporting lifecycle security for home and industrial applications founded on voluntary, industry-driven international standards."

23. "Consumer Reports Launches Digital Standard to Safeguard Consumers' Security and Privacy in Complex Marketplace," press release, *Consumer Reports* Media Room, March 6, 2017, http://consumerreports.org/media-room/press-releases/2017/03 /consumer_reports_launches_digital_standard_to_safeguard_consumers_security _and_privacy_in_complex_marketplace.

24. Spamhaus Malware Labs, "Spamhaus Botnet Threat Report 2017," Spamhaus, January 1, 2018, http://spamhaus.org/news/article/772/spamhaus-botnet-threat -report-2017.

25. Kathleen Richards, "Botnet Takedowns: A Dramatic Defense," *Search Security* (blog), TechTarget, March 2013, https://searchsecurity.techtarget.com/feature/Botnet -takedowns-A-dramatic-defense.

26. Jason Healey, "Innovation on Cyber Collaboration: Leverage at Scale," Atlantic Council, May 2018, http://atlanticcouncil.org/images/publications/Innovation-Cyber -WEB.pdf.

27. Ibid.

ABOUT THE AUTHORS

Jason Healey is a senior research scholar at Columbia University's School for International and Public Affairs specializing in cyber conflict, competition, and cooperation. Prior to this, he was the founding director of the Cyber Statecraft Initiative at the Atlantic Council, where he remains a senior fellow. He has worked for Goldman Sachs, including as an executive director in Hong Kong. As director for cyber infrastructure protection at the White House from 2003 to 2005, he advised President George W. Bush and coordinated U.S. efforts to secure U.S. cyberspace and critical infrastructure. From 2001 to 2003 he served as vice chairman of the Financial Services Information Sharing and Analysis Center. Healey started his career in the U.S. Air Force, earning two Meritorious Service Medals for his early work in cyber operations at Headquarters Air Force at the Pentagon and as a founding member of the Joint Task Force–Computer Network Defense, the world's first joint cyber warfighting unit. He has been a lecturer in cyber policy at Georgetown University and in cyber national security studies at Johns Hopkins University's School of Advanced International Studies.

Healy is the editor of *A Fierce Domain: Cyber Conflict, 1986 to 2012* and coauthor of *Cyber Security Policy Guidebook*. His articles and essays have been published by think tanks including the Aspen Strategy Group, Atlantic Council, and National Research Council, and academic journals from Brown and Georgetown Universities, among others. He is a member of the Defense Science Board Task Force on Cyber Deterrence and president of the Cyber Conflict Studies Association. Healy has degrees from the U.S. Air Force Academy in political science, from Johns Hopkins University in liberal arts, and from James Madison University in information security.

Robert K. Knake is a senior fellow for cyber policy at the Council on Foreign Relations (CFR). He is also a senior research scientist at Northeastern University's Global Resilience Institute. Knake served from 2011 to 2015 as director for cybersecurity policy at the National Security Council. In this role, he was responsible for the development of presidential policy on cybersecurity and built and managed federal processes for cyber incident response and vulnerability management. Before joining government, Knake was an international affairs fellow at CFR.

Knake's publications include *Cyber War: The Next Threat to National Security and What to Do About It* and the CFR Council Special Report *Internet Governance in an Age of Cyber Insecurity*. He has testified before Congress on cybersecurity information sharing and on the problem of attribution in cyberspace, and written and lectured extensively on cybersecurity policy. Knake holds undergraduate degrees in history and government from Connecticut College and a master's degree in public policy from the Harvard Kennedy School.

ADVISORY COMMITTEE
Zero Botnets

David Altshuler
TechFoundation

Chris B. Baker
Dyn Inc.

Chris Boyer
AT&T

Fred H. Cate
Indiana University

Benjamin Dean
Iconoclast Tech LLC

Matthew Eggers
U.S. Chamber of Commerce

Kristen E. Eichensehr
*University of California,
Los Angeles School of Law*

Ben Flatgard
JP Morgan Chase & Co.

Margie Gilbert
Team Cymru, Inc.

Ryan M. Gillis
Palo Alto Networks

Nathaniel J. Gleicher
Facebook

Brittan Heller
Anti-Defamation League

Cameron F. Kerry
Brookings Institution

Jongsun A. Kim
*U.S. Senate Select Committee
on Intelligence*

Douglas J. Kramer
Cloudflare, Inc.

Michael Kuiken
Office of Senator Charles Schumer

This report reflects the judgments and recommendations of the authors. It does not necessarily represent the views of members of the advisory committee, whose involvement should in no way be interpreted as an endorsement of the report by either themselves or the organizations with which they are affiliated.

Sanjay Parekh
Prototype Prime

Mira Patel
Chan Zuckerberg Initiative

Jonathan Sondik Perelman
ICM Partners

Neal A. Pollard
PricewaterhouseCoopers LLP

Brendan P. Shields
U.S. House of Representatives

Megan Stifel
Silicon Harbor Consultants, LLC

Michael Sulmeyer
*Harvard Kennedy School's
Belfer Center for Science
and International Affairs*

Frederick H. Tsai
salesforce.com, inc.

Ira Winkler
Secure Mentem

Evan D. Wolff
Crowell & Moring LLP

JD Work
*Columbia University's School
of International and Public Affairs*